The Clay Jar

Also by
Caroline Giles Banks

Warm Under the Cat:
Haiku and Senryu Poems

The Clock Chimes:
Haiku and Senryu Poems

The Weight of Whiteness:
A Memoir in Poetry

The Clay Jar

Haiku, Senryu
and
Haibun Poems

by Caroline Giles Banks

WELLINGTON-GILES PRESS

Minneapolis, Minnesota
United States of America

WELLINGTON-GILES PRESS
4040 Sheridan Avenue South
Minneapolis, Minnesota 55410
United States of America
wellingtongilespress@gmail.com

Book design by Cate Hubbard
Sumi-e art by Lili Hipp

Library of Congress Control Number : 2013939710

ISBN 978-0-9645254-4-3
eBook ISBN 978-0-9645254-6-7

For my teachers

awake at night—
the sound of the water jar
cracking in the cold

– Matsuo Bashō

Contents

I

II

I

Haiku and Senryu

thunderbolt
the digital clock flashes
12, 12, 12

after the torrent
the all clear
cicadas

gardening
in the roots of a weed
a silver horseshoe charm

waiting
to go home
motionless clouds

tree limb gone
so, too, its shadow
on the window shade

tree cutting
the robin keeps returning
to the stump

fireflies
4th of July sparklers
fireflies

my neighbor's
tap, tap, tap
summer flees

raking leaves
before the photo shoot
instant summer

first day of autumn
the geese
so sure of the way

Japanese tourists
fly to Canada
maple viewing time

come in
with winter
cricket's sound

winter winds
in my driveway
three Christmas trees

Epiphany
fishermen sit
by holes in the lake

less pesticides
more monarchs
noisy spring

first day of spring
leg hairs
mat the razor

Fuji in fog
the bus driver lectures
on the mountain's suicides

watch out, shōgun,
tourists coming
nightingale's song

that jack pine
new companion
in this old solitude

baby storks
clack their beaks
rooftop castanets

trade rat
a lost ring returned
for barley-n-oats

communion
I think of
last night's tryst

communion
on the priest's wrist
Mickey Mouse

TGIF
the priest leaves the hospital
humming a tune

eviction notice
Adam and Eve sculpture packed
in the apple crate

first Sunday in Lent
Girl Scouts deliver
Thin Mints

Jesus Saves bus
out of gas
on the freeway

religion: *none*
just a picture hook
on my hospital room wall

his side: army cap
her side: church decal
car window war and peace

the woman in 8F
her prayer book tucked inside
the safety brochure

tossing Buddha one more coin
the incense stick
finally lights

garden shop
all the Buddhas
on clearance

feel the warmth
of Bashō's frogpond
just Xeroxed

haiku workshop
on cadence and beat
the clock chimes

Japan aftershocks
so many
haiku

bankruptcy
the
judge
asks
if
the
poems
have
value

Barnes and Noble
the cop browses
in *True Crimes*

convicted felon
hesitating to buy
her lifestyle magazine

TV sage
lectures on
silent meditation

poster
in
dermatologist's
waiting
room—
Sun
Showers

Kabuki actors
take their bows
pansies in the breeze

Duane Hanson's *Tourists*
another gallery guest
asks if I'm real

far from England
yet tonight
a Turner sky

magnetic
word
falls
to
the
kitchen
floor—
sweep

this writer's
cross
a gold pen

parkarma

new haiku
warm
under the cat

the cat's tail
swishes   aside
an entire semester's work

silent fog
cat fur
everywhere

cat gone for good
turning off the radio
when leaving home

birthday party
my lover's wife brings
the prettiest flowers

slip of the tongue
he kisses
my *nickels*

his turn to cook
again he can't find
the thyme

checking out the blond
he forgets to buy
the *My True Love* card

B&B *honeymoon* suite
for the first time we talk
of separation

extra valentine
thinking of
my ex

address book
in the *Ms* my ex's
shirt and shorts size

the moon
my heart
both full

all the holidays
in mother's
dresser drawer

on the mother-of-the-bride's
bedside stand
wilted cucumber slices

distant father
all the kids pass him
their artichoke hearts

Father's Day
in the park
balls everywhere

LD son's note
about his drug problem
not one spelling mistake

chemical health notes
misreading *IV*
as the Roman numeral

middle school cast party
Cinderella bullies
the prince

the girl with the shiner
on her purse
the peace sign

the weaver's spirit
travels the thread
in and out of the rug

museum teepee
cobwebs crisscross
the smoke hole

Columbus Day
Indian paintbrush
line the parade route

12/20/12
buying the 2013 calendar
anyway

forgotten
the bills accrue fines
in the prehistoric pot

another 100-year flood
not shaking
the rainstick

war imminent
reading aloud, louder
Rumi's love poems

too much war
changing the channel
to *Reality TV*

9/11 migration
wondering what else
the geese know

peace vigil
the candle from
our *Ready Response* kit

more anthrax
eating all the chocolate
from our survival cache

paper cranes sag
on the weeping willow
fine rain

State of the Union
the eagle circles
its prey

war declared
in the Middle East
tonight a crescent moon

Afghan refugee camp
vultures follow
Red Crescent workers

CNN News
the Somali boy wears
my son's old tee

Armenian lace doily
blown by *perestroika*
East to West

weathervane
the peace dove oscillates
West/East   East/West

Ozone Action Day
sailboats race
into grayness

ice saves
Florida's citrus crops
guest workers freeze

99¢ baskets
the girl's childhood
in each bent reed

beside the story
on modern slavery
an ad for the Ritz

World AIDS Day
a full page ad
for Viagra

ambulance siren
guest workers
duck for cover

50th birthday bouquet
the rose drops
its last petal

50-something
curriculum vitae still
only two pages

the carousel spins
defining myself
all over again

last season's outerwear
heaped for recycling
snakeskins

Labor Day
filing for
unemployment compensation

job hunting
into today's mail
Welcome to AARP card

new job
an employee number inked
on my wrist

career counselor
a *clearance* tag stuck
to the sole of her shoe

Life Changes seminar
the new member clutches
her teddy bear

driver's license
for the first time ever
my weight is the same

sleeping in
the answering machine says
I'm out

heart trouble
in the car
sneaking cheese

angiogram
my broken heart
undetected

waiting in the ER
the hospital flag
at half staff

widowed
growing my hair long
the way he liked it

Mayo Clinic
all the parking marked
handicapped

wedding march steps
getting to know
my two new knees

feeling better
editing signage
on the ICU ward

misplaced dictionary
forgetting how to spell
Alzheimer's

last oak leaf
asking after
my father's health

Yaktrax on Bearskin Lake
diamonds
on the soles of her shoes

      (For Hillary, 1969-1994)

the clay jar
some day
holding me

II

Haibun

Layover
Narita, Japan

1

Arriving just before dark at the Buddhist temple in the old section of Narita I find the grounds are open but the numerous buildings have closed for the night.

temple
buildings
closed
wondering
what
path
to
take

2

In the temple courtyard a couple throws sticks of incense into a stone brazier. Cupping our hands, we rinse our faces with aromatic smoke.

jasmine
thrown
to
Buddha
returned
as
smoke

3

Paths through gardens and woods take me to a large, ancient tree where I add to the incense sticks and other offerings tucked into its lower branches and gnarled roots. A Buddha sits in the fork of an upper branch.

myself
not
myself
under
the
sacred
tree

Taliesin
Spring Green, Wisconsin

1

Taliesin, the former home and studio of the architect,
Frank Lloyd Wright, is in the Wisconsin River valley
near the town of Spring Green. Touring the estate in
mid-September, I do not see the house the first time I
drive past the stone entrance gate. Painted in sandstone
yellow, sumac red, and tree trunk brown, the house
nestles into the hillside.

not seeing
the famous architect's house
my urban eye

2

Frank Lloyd Wright brought antiquities from Japan to
Taliesin. He insisted on placing many of them in the
gardens where he could view them as he walked. He
believed that the beauty of an art object or architectural
structure lies in its relation to the natural world.

ting! ting! ting!
acorns bounce off
the temple bell

3

Taliesin, built in the early 1900s and rebuilt after
several major fires is, like many other Frank Lloyd
Wright buildings, falling apart. The house foundation
and walls are cracked and apprentice architects
affiliated with the Frank Lloyd Wright Fellowship work
on repairing a leaky roof.

architect and water
take turns
working the stone

Madeline Island
Lake Superior, Wisconsin

1

Madeline Island, the largest of the Apostle Islands, is located in the southwest corner of Lake Superior. Indigenous tribes, French Voyageurs engaged in the fur trade, and Catholic and Anglican missionaries frequented the island in past centuries. Today Madeline Island is the destination of summer day-trippers, folks with cabins, and the crews of yachts that sail the Great Lakes. Generations of animals and birds have witnessed these changing human migrations on and off the island.

the screen door bangs
on the boarded up fish house
gulls wheel and scream

2

Well-worn paths through the old Indian burial grounds
suggest many visitors. Native peoples come to these
burial grounds to honor their deceased relatives,
placing ritual offerings of flowers and food in front of
some of the graves.

ants, too, enjoy
the dish of wild berries
beside the headstone

feathers, sweet grass,
even an ermine skin—
gifts for the journey home

3

On a recent visit to the island a sign, *BAD RIVER INDIAN RESERVATION. NO TRESPASSING*, stops me at the cemetery gate. An antler with feathers is secured to the chain and lock. Tall bluestem grasses, spreading sumac, and wild flowers cover the paths and tombstones.

burial grounds
now closed to tourists
Indian paintbrush everywhere

Notes

Page 18: "less pesticides," refers to Rachael Carson's book, *Silent Spring* (1962), in which she condemns the use of pesticides hazardous to wildlife.

Page 19: "watch out, shōgun," refers to the Nijo Castle's "nightingale floors" which were designed to squeak when walked on, thus alerting the guards to any intruders.

Page 22: "eviction notice," First Place Award—Haiku. The League of Minnesota Poets' Poetry Contest, 2003.

Page 26: "feel the warmth," Runner-up: Gerald P. Brady Memorial Senryu Contest, Haiku Society of America, 1988.

Page 35: "his turn to cook," Runner-up: Senryu. Kaji Aso Studio. Boston Haiku Society Second Annual Haiku Contest, 1989.

Page 42: "12/20/12," refers to the Mayan prediction that the world will end on 12/21/12.

Page 45: "paper cranes sag," refers to Hiroshima Remembrance Day. Every August 6th people gather at the Lake Harriet Peace Garden in Minneapolis, Minnesota to remember the bombing of Hiroshima, Japan by the United States. Based on the true story of Sadako Sasaki and the thousand paper cranes, origami cranes are hung on trees in the garden in the continuing hope for world peace.

Page 45: "State of the Union," refers to President George W. Bush's address on January 28, 2003 in which he outlined justification for the 2003 invasion of Iraq.

Page 58: "Yaktrax on Bearskin Lake," refers to Paul Simon's song entitled, "Diamonds on the Soles of Her Shoes." This haiku is dedicated to Hillary (1969-1994) who, as a girl, camped, swam, paddled, skied, snowshoed, and loved life on Bearskin Lake, located in Minnesota's Superior National Forest.

Acknowledgments

The author would like to acknowledge the editors of the following anthologies, journals and magazines for publishing the poems listed below, some in slightly modified form. Copyright © by Caroline Giles Banks.

Caroline Giles Banks, "after the torrent," *frogpond* 11, no.3 (August 1988). And in *Modern Haiku* 26, no.3 (fall 1995).

—, "waiting," *Haiku Quarterly* 3, no.3 (autumn 1991).

—, "first day of autumn," *Haiku Quarterly* 2, no.3 (autumn 1990). And in *Now This: Contemporary Poems of Beginnings, Renewals, and Firsts*, ed. Robert Epstein. Shelbyville, KY: Wasteland Press, 2013.

—, "come in," *Haiku Quarterly* 1, no.4 (winter 1989).

—, "winter winds," *Brussels Sprout, a haiku journal* 5, no.1 (May 1988).

—, "epiphany," *Brussels Sprout, a haiku journal* 5, no.1 (May 1988). And in *Modern Haiku* 26, no.3 (fall 1995).

—, "communion," in *Midwest Haiku Anthology*, eds. Randy M. Brooks and Lee Gurga. Decatur, Illinois: High/Coo Press, 1992. And in *Modern Haiku* 21, no.1 (winter-spring 1990). And in *Modern Haiku* 26, no.3 (fall 1995).

—, "TGIF," *Modern Haiku* 35, no.3 (autumn 2004).

—, " tossing Buddha one more coin," in *The Sacred in Contemporary Haiku*, ed. Robert Epstein. Createspace, 2014.

—, "feel the warmth of," *frogpond* 11, no.2 (May 1988). And in *A Haiku Path. The Haiku Society of America* 1968-1988. The Haiku Society of America, Inc., 1994.

—, "bankruptcy," *frogpond* 23, no.1 (2000).

—, "TV sage," *Potpourri: A Magazine of the Literary Arts* 10, no.4 (1998).

—,"Kabuki actors," in *A Solitary Leaf: 1996 Members' Anthology. Haiku Society of America*, eds. Randy M. Brooks and Lee Gurga. Decatur, Illinois: Brooks Books, 1997.

—,"far from England," *frogpond* 11. No.3 (August 1988).

—,"magnetic," *frogpond* 23, no.1 (2000).

—,"new haiku," *Haiku Quarterly* 1, no.1 (spring 1989).

—,"the cat's tail," *The Southwest Journal* (fall 1993).

—,"silent fog," in *dreams wander*, eds. Nina A. Wicker, Peggy Willis Lyles, Kenneth C. Leibman. New York: Haiku Society of America, 1994.

—,"his turn to cook," in *Haiku for Lovers*, ed. Manu Bazzano. London: MQ Publications, 2003. Also in *Midwest Haiku Anthology*, eds. Randy M. Brooks and Lee Gurga. Decatur, Illinois: High/Coo Press, 1992. And in *Haiku World: An International Poetry Almanac*, ed. William J. Higginson. Tokyo, New York and London: Kodansha International, 1996.

—,"extra valentine," *Potpourri: A Magazine of the Literary Arts* 10, no.3 (1998).

—,"LD son's note," *Dharma Review* (August 1993).

—,"all the holidays," *Haiku Quarterly* 3, no.3 (autumn 1991).

—,"museum teepee," *Potpourri: A Magazine of the Literary Arts* 10, no.3 (1998).

—,"another 100-year flood," *frogpond* 20, no.2 (September 1997).

—,"war imminent," *frogpond* 14, no.2 (summer 1991).

—,"too much war," *Haiku Society of America Members' Anthology* 2003, ed. David G. Lanone. Haiku Society of America, 2003.

—,"9/11 migration," *frogpond* 25, no. 3 (2002).

—,"peace vigil," *Acorn. a journal of contemporary haiku* 13 (fall 2004).

—,"more anthrax," *frogpond* 25, no.3 (2002).

—,"paper cranes sag," *Potpourri: A Magazine of the Literary Arts* 10, no.3 (1998). And in *Potpourri: A Magazine of the Literary Arts* 11, no.1 (1999).

—,"State of the Union," in *Walking The Same Path. Haiku Society of America 2004 Members' Anthology*, ed. Connie Post. Haiku Society of America, 2004.

—,"Ozone Action Day," *Potpourri: A Magazine of the Literary Arts* 10, no.2 (1998).

—,"99¢ baskets," *Modern Haiku* 26, no.3 (fall 1995).

—,"50th birthday bouquet," *frogpond* 18, no.2 (summer 1995).

—,"50-something," *frogpond* 18, no.2 (summer 1995).

—,"the carousel spins," *Dragonfly. East/West Haiku Quarterly* 15, no.2 (spring 1989).

—,"job hunting," *frogpond* 18, no.2 (summer 1995).

—,"new job," in *Now This: Contemporary Poems of Beginnings, Renewals, and Firsts*, ed. Robert Epstein. Shelbyville, KY: Wasteland Press, 2013.

—,"heart trouble," *Brussels Sprout, a haiku journal* 5, no.1 (May 1988).

—,"waiting in the ER," in *One Breath. Haiku Society of America 1995 Members' Anthology*, eds. Jean Dubois, Michael McNierney and Elizabeth L. Nichols. New York: Haiku Society of America, 1996.

—,"wedding march steps," in *bits of itself. The Haiku Society of America Membership Anthology 2002*, eds. Jerry Ball, Naia and Wendy Wright. HSA Publications, 2003. And in *Now This: Contemporary Poems of Beginnings, Renewals, and Firsts*, ed. Robert Epstein. Shelbyville, KY: Wasteland Press, 2013.

—,"the clay jar," in *Midwest Haiku Anthology,* eds. Randy M. Brooks and Lee Gurga. Decatur, Illinois: High/Coo Press, 1992. And in *Modern Haiku* 20, no.1 (winter-spring 1989). And in *Modern Haiku* 26, no.3 (fall 1995).

—,"ants, too, enjoy," *frogpond* 15, no.2 (fall-winter 1992).

Epigraph

Haiku of Basho's ["Awake at night-"; p. 19] from THE ESSENTIAL HAIKU: VERSIONS OF BASHO, BUSON & ISSA, EDITED AND WITH AN INTRODUCTION by ROBERT HASS. Introduction and selection copyright © 1994 by Robert Hass. Unless otherwise noted, all translations copyright © 1994 by Robert Hass. Reprinted by permission of HarperCollins Publishers.

Back Cover

Dee Evetts, reprinted, with changes, from *frogpond* 25, no.3 (2002), by permission of the author.

R. W. Grandinetti Rader, reprinted, with changes, from *frogpond* 11, no.2 (May 1988), by permission of the editor.

Robert Spiess, reprinted, with changes, from *Modern Haiku* 26, no.3 (fall 1995), by permission of the editor.

About the Author

Caroline Giles Banks, born in Boston, Massachusetts, was educated at Wellesley College, the University of New Mexico, the University of Minnesota, and the University of Chicago. Dr. Banks is a cultural anthropologist by training and profession and was on the faculties of the University of Wisconsin-River Falls and Luther College in Decorah, Iowa. She is the author of *Warm Under the Cat: Haiku and Senryu Poems, The Clock Chimes: Haiku and Senryu Poems*, and *The Weight of Whiteness: A Memoir in Poetry*. Her award-winning poems have been published in numerous anthologies, literary magazines and journals. She lives in Minneapolis, Minnesota.

www.ingramcontent.com/pod-product-compliance
Lightning Source LLC
Chambersburg PA
CBHW051044030426
42339CB00006B/197